SOLO TIME FOR STRINGS
BOOK II

Solo	Page	Assigned (√)	Grade
Country Dance	1		
Bohemian Folk Songs	2		
Dutch Dance	3		
Americana	4		
Israeli Songs	5		
American Songs	6		
Songs of Many Lands	7		
Hiawatha	8		
The Brook	9		
Christmas Songs I	10		
Christmas Songs II	11		
English Melodies	12		
French Songs	13		
Scottish Songs	14		
Crinoline and Lace	15		
Russian Melodies	16		
Religioso	17		
A Swiss Miss	18		
American Dance	19		
Irish Folk Songs	20		
Mexican Songs	21		
Italian Folk Songs	22		
Czech Folk Songs	23		
String Along	24		

D1245290

THE INSTRUMENT AND BOW

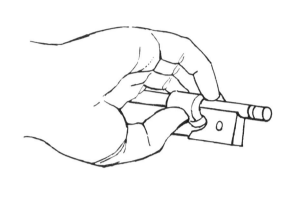

#2

Notice the curved thumb and the curved little finger.

Pizzicato

Place the tip of the right thumb on the corner of the fingerboard.

Pluck the string sideways with the first finger about an inch from the end of the fingerboard.

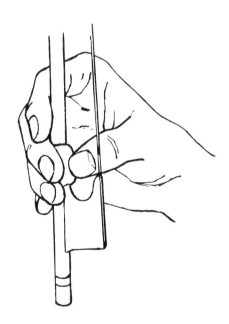

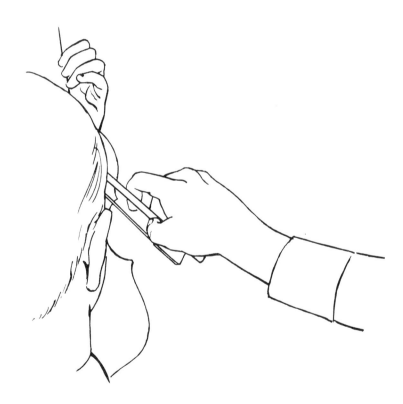

#1

The tip of the curved thumb is on the stick or thumb grip next to the frog.

The curved thumb touches the side of the hair near the frog.

The second finger is opposite the curved thumb.

The first finger rests on top of the stick between the 1st and 2nd joints.

The little finger, also curved, rests on top of the stick.

#3

The thumb is opposite the second finger, forming a circle.

The first finger rests on the stick between the 1st and 2nd joints.

THE INSTRUMENT AND BOW

Posture and Position

Both feet should be on the floor.
The left foot is forward.
Sit on the front third of the chair.
Lean forward, away from the back of the chair.
Direct the bow between the knees.

The left elbow is centered.
The thumb is underneath the neck to receive the downward pressure of the finger tips.
The finger tips press the string firmly.
The left wrist is well out, straight or with a graceful outward curve.

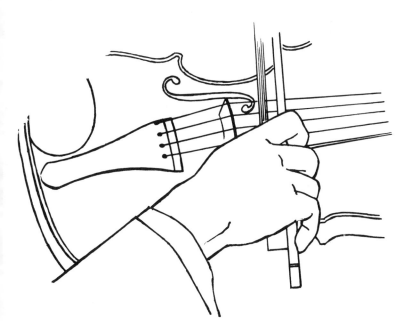

1
Beginning of the down bow.
All fingers are curved.

2
End of the down bow, beginning of the up bow...all fingers are slightly curved. Note the lowered wrist.

Orchestra Members . . .

LEARN: DAILY PRACTICE ROUTINE... should include the following:

I. The "pressed" bow, 2 - 4 - 8 - 12 - 16 - 20 to a bow

II. The "stopped" bow, 2 - 4 - 8 - 12 - 16 - 20 to a bow

III. Play all fingers in the 2 - 3 pattern and in the 1 - 2 pattern on all strings, single bows, slur 2, slur 3, slur 4.

IV. Review one of the DAILY DRILLS such as "keeping fingers down", etc.

V. Review 1 previously learned solo. Practice 2 new solos.

VI. For each selection: 1. Practice the bowing pattern on the open string.
2. Review, mentally, the finger pattern for the key signature as learned in Solo Time, Book I and in the Workbook I & II.

LEARN: COUNTING TIME

A system of counting time is most essential to develop reading ability. An ability to play a piece of music at first sight is a goal for which every young musician should strive. Through improvement in reading ability, most of your practice and attention may be devoted to good intonation, good bowing, and playing expressively.

Tapping the foot is a definite aid in learning various rhythm patterns. The diagram below shows the relationship of the foot to a rhythm pattern.

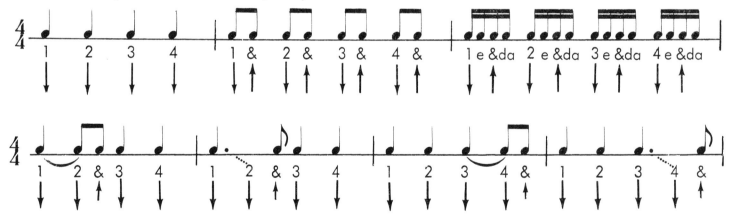

Practice the above by tapping the foot and counting aloud. Pay attention to the position of the foot as each note is counted. Tap your foot "down" on the "beat" and "up" on the "and." You may also clap the hands to indicate the rhythm as you tap the foot and count aloud.

COUNTRY DANCE

BOWING PATTERN: (typical of the bowing-rhythm pattern that should be practiced for most selections)

BOHEMIAN FOLK SONGS

DUTCH DANCE

Moderato

Ritard

AMERICANA

ISRAELI SONGS

HATIKVOH

6

AMERICAN SONGS

SWEET BETSY FROM PIKE

HOME ON THE RANGE

SONGS OF MANY LANDS

AMERICA

ALL THROUGH THE NIGHT

PRAYER OF THANKSGIVING

8

HIAWATHA

THE BROOK

CHRISTMAS SONGS I

GOOD KING WENCESLAS

ANGELS WE HAVE HEARD ON HIGH

THE FIRST NOEL

CHRISTMAS SONGS II

ENGLISH MELODIES

FRENCH SONGS

SCOTTISH SONGS

CRINOLINE AND LACE

RUSSIAN MELODIES

VOLGA BOATMAN

CHANSON TRISTE

RELIGIOSO

BENEATH THY GUIDING HAND

CRUSADERS' HYMN

ONWARD CHRISTIAN SOLDIERS

A SWISS MISS

AMERICAN DANCE

20

IRISH FOLK SONGS

THE MINSTREL BOY

THE IRISH WASHERWOMAN

MEXICAN SONGS

BEAUTIFUL HEAVEN

CLAP HANDS DANCE

ITALIAN FOLK SONGS

CZECH FOLK SONGS

STRING ALONG